GOD
IS WITH US

D1367299

GOD
IS WITH US

Rediscovering

the Meaning

of Christmas

F. THOMAS TROTTER

UPPER
ROOM BOOKS
NASHVILLE

God Is with Us: Rediscovering the Meaning of Christmas

Copyright © 1997 by Nashville Banner Publishing Company.
All Rights Reserved.

Cover Direction: Michelle Wetherbee
Cover Design: Laura Beers
Interior Design: Susan Hulme
First Printing: September 1997 (5)

The Upper Room Web Site: http://www.upperoom.org

Printed in the United States of America

Library of Congress Cataloging-in-Publication Data

Trotter, F. Thomas (Frederick Thomas), 1926-
        God is with us: rediscovering the meaning of
        Christmas / by F. Thomas Trotter.
        p.   cm.
        *"Most of the reflections in this book were written at Christmastime over the
        last decade and first published in the Nashville Banner"*– Preface.
        ISBN 0-8358-0813-0 (pbk.)
        1. Christmas.   I. Nashville banner.   II. Title.
    BV45.T75   1997
    263'.915—dc21   97-10328
                                                         CIP

Dedication

For Gania

Contents

Preface

*T*his is another book about Christmas. There is no other holiday in the calendar that is more celebrated than this one. But I have noticed over the years that Christmas is a time with many different meanings. Powerful emotions and memories gather around the day.

There are other holidays that seem to have their own reasons for being. Birthdays and anniversaries come to mind. But the many layers of the meaning of Christmas seem to be endlessly evocative. Of all the holy days of the Christian calendar, Christmas seems the most uncomplicated on the surface. We celebrate the day by recreating what we know of the first Christmas. Gift giving with all of its tinsel and affection repeats the tradition of the gifts of the Magi—the wise men from the east.

We enjoy a big family meal if we are able to afford the luxury. That tradition became established in the middle ages and is remembered in the rich carols of English

Christmas. These are the available and accustomed features of the holiday. What we do not always reflect upon is the fact that the heart of Christmas is the most mysterious and dramatic assertion in Christian belief. That claim is this: God becomes one of us. The divine takes on our flesh with all its temptations and frailty. In most of the religious systems of the world, humans become gods. Only in Christianity is the daring claim made that God becomes human.

The whole system of Christian life and ethics is grounded in this great affirmation. We sing about this mystery in the great Christmas hymns. Often we sing without much reflection on the profound mystery of the Incarnation. "Veiled in flesh the Godhead see; hail th' incarnate Deity, pleased with us in flesh to dwell, Jesus, our Emmanuel." That's rich material for reflection.

When I write about religion, I have in mind the reader who may have grown up in the church but have misgivings about reconciling religious belief and secular attitudes. We live in a time that is not unfriendly toward religion, but indifferent. It is my belief that the story of God's way with women and men is the central theme of a happy life. Examining that theme is the purpose of these reflections and of this book.

Most of the reflections in this book were written at Christmastime over the last decade and first published in the *Nashville Banner*. Irby Simpkins Jr., the publisher of the *Banner*, generously makes it possible for me to write a weekly column for the paper's forum pages. These reflections are used with his permission.

F. Thomas Trotter

GOD IS WITH US

Foreward

*L*ast Christmas I received a Christmas tree ornament from a special friend. In a handwritten note on the enclosure card, my friend wrote meaningfully that this was "so token a present" to symbolize so deep a friendship.

I treasure the Christmas ornament because of its beauty and distinctiveness. However, I treasure it even more because, in some mysterious way, it symbolizes the gift of self which my friend gave to me in that present.

In some mysterious way, this is the theme of Tom Trotter's book of Advent and Christmas meditations, *God Is with Us: Rediscovering the Meaning of Christmas*. In these twenty-five brief reflections, Trotter invites us to meditate on the heart of the Christmas message: God's gift to us at Christmas is God's self in a baby, the most vulnerable being imaginable. The gift that God calls us to give to others is ourselves, in care, love, and vulnerability—the risking of one's self for the sake of God, others, and self.

I invite you to allow yourself time to meditate and to live with these reflections, deceptive in the simplicity and directness of their words. Simple and direct: words that point to the reality of God's gift of the baby Jesus.

Our time in history, Trotter points out, is more indifferent than unfriendly toward religion. At Christmas, indifference is most frequently expressed in our inability to understand and express that deep truth of Christmas that "the true gift of Christmas lies behind the gift . . . The gift that changes lives and makes for new community is the gift of self . . . To give oneself to others—parents, children, neighbors, those in need of us—is the gift that ultimately gives Christmas its magic and its power."

I invite you to give yourself to others without expecting or asking for anything in return. That's what it means to live out of the essence of giving and receiving. A quartet of singers under the lighted tree in Rockefeller Center Plaza on Manhattan's Fifth Avenue expresses that mysterious reality, Trotter says. "We don't represent anybody; we're not raising money. We just want to give a Christmas gift to the city."

The baby Jesus was the gift of God's vulnerability to us, the sign of God's love for the world which could hardly return any expectation that an all-powerful, all-wise, and all-loving God might have for it. And in some mysterious way, we are called to give our gift of self and of love to a world of persons living in fear, dislocation, and in need of hope.

As Tom Trotter leads us to focus upon the gift of ourselves to others at Christmas, he asks us to ponder the truth of Christmas which is "the theme of all the great religions that those without food or shelter or rights or privilege have a claim on those who do have those things." As a response to the "politics of indifference," in Jesus' day and in ours, the theme of Christmas is God's care for those who have been without care. "Why else would the story be framed in the fragile forms of the helpless . . . young parents fleeing from political violence, an infant born in a stable, placed in an animal's feeding trough, and visited by the herdsmen who sense the presence of hope?"

In *God Is with Us*, Trotter offers to us that important God-given gift, the gift of imagination. To live imaginatively, as the author uses the word, is a moral act of putting ourselves in the place of another person. The outrageous suggestion that God "by a mighty act of imagination came to live with us as a helpless baby" is at the heart of the Christmas story. "Christian theology suggests that God's act of imagination in the Incarnation needs to be answered by risking ourselves in imagining the being of others in need of hope." Can our own experience of family and community be enlarged as we imagine in our hearts and act through our wills to give ourselves to others at a deeper level of our vulnerability and their need than we have done in the past?

❦

Tom Trotter has been a friend and a mentor to me over many years, during his time as General Secretary of the Board of Higher Education of The United Methodist Church and as President of Alaska Pacific University. The opportunity to write this brief introduction to *God Is with Us* is a genuine gift to me. I hope I can follow the lead he gives to live and act more imaginatively as I go out to others, near and far, this Christmas. That, in turn, will be my gift to him.

Rosemary Keller
Union Theological Seminary
New York City

Christmas: The Tug of Belief

*P*olls suggest that people don't trust many of the institutions that have long held their confidence. In fact, we live in a time of vast skepticism. Politicians have disappointed us. Journalists affect the sensational over the informative style of reporting. Even the judicial system has been battered by long and inconclusive televised trials. The habits of fear persist in our dealings with other nations after a half-century of Cold War. We find it difficult to tell fact from fancy, reality from realism, and truth from dissimulation.

Now comes the Christmas season. This is the most memorable time in the year for the Christian community. Christmas is the celebration of the coming of Jesus into the world. But it too has been affected by the erosion of skepticism. A vast and dreary commercialism has overwhelmed the simple shapes of the sweet holiday of the birth. Lost in the fury of the celebration is the reason for the celebration.

GOD IS WITH US

Many think that Christmas is just another one of those lovely things that has been put away in this world's attic. A fresh look at the story will reveal how contemporary the Christmas story really is. The world we know is remarkably like the world of the Christmas story.

In our world, poverty is the norm rather than the exception. The Christmas story is a narrative about poor people. The story is not only about poor people, but poor people caught up in bureaucracy. Mary and Joseph were forced to travel to a distant city to satisfy bureaucratic regulations. It was important to take a census so that taxes could be assessed. Sound familiar?

Mary was pregnant before she married Joseph. She probably had been subject to gossip and scorn. Traditions from the medieval church suggest that Joseph himself was confused. Although Mary knew of the wondrous mystery of her pregnancy, she would carry the stigma of what we call today an "unwed mother." A suspicious innkeeper suggested it would be better for them to stay in the barn instead of a warm, inside room. Oh yes, he assured them the inn was already sold out. Sound familiar?

The couple with the newborn baby were told that they were under suspicion of the government. Herod the king threatened to slaughter all male infants to remove the presumed threat of a political rival. So the family fled their homeland. They became refugees. They were actually fleeing genocide. Sound familiar?

So much for the sweetness of the first Christmas. Put on glasses that can penetrate the sentimental legends of Christmas and find that it was a hard, desperate, and fearful time. We need look no further than our own

GOD IS WITH US

neighborhoods to find analogies to the Gospel narrative.

Many modern folk have an uneasy relationship with Christmas. Skepticism suggests it is merely a nostalgic and disposable holiday. But Christmas can be a time of tumbled emotions. Psychiatrists tell us that a common experience of the holiday is fear and anxiety.

The setting of the first Christmas was also a time of fear, anxiety, and hopelessness. When we don't recognize that, we may even labor under some guilt that we feel anxiety at Christmas. But through that curtain of desperation came the shout of the angel chorus with the remarkable words: "Do not be afraid!" (Luke 2:10).

"Perfect love casts out fear" (1 John 4:18). This is no abstract principle. We understand it through the mixed emotions of a family Christmas. We sense it when we extend our care to others in need. We proclaim it when we recall the ancient meaning of the Christian proclamation that "God is with us" (Matt. 1:23). For centuries, confidence in this assertion has made hope possible.

But the tug of belief as a response to a world full of fear and distrust pulls us toward Christmas. Even the most skeptical and cynical feel some stirrings at the season. The story is the announcement that the love of God is now loosed in the world. Love has overcome fear, and the world will never be the same again.

❦

*T*he reality
of love makes
giving possible.

The Unexplainable Gift

Only Scrooge doesn't like Christmas. But he finally comes to his senses before Charles Dickens's famous story is over. Christmas contains so much that is important to us. The stuff of Christmas includes families, friends, memories, hopes, and dreams.

Our family has recorded Christmas celebrations with a feast of phototaking. Some future historian, finding the cache of pictures, might assume that we always were decorated that way. For most of us, Christmas is a time of family bonding.

The giving and receiving of gifts is the major ritual activity at Christmas. The excitement of anticipation is a wonderful dimension of the day for the children.

One of my children always had a system of guessing the gifts by Christmas Eve. She used her considerable powers of reasoning to determine by shape, location, wrapping, weight, and parental reaction just what was in every package. This activity is also pleasurable to adults. They are likely to have the same sense of excitement, although tempered by the responsibilities of the day.

Gift giving is a joyful and wonderful activity. Its deeper significance, of course, stems from the recollection of the first Christmas when the Magi from the East brought gifts to the Christ Child. So the giving and receiving of gifts is a symbolic act as well as an act of joy and love.

The reality of love makes giving possible. Gift giving, then, is a sign of the meaning of a human relationship. The gifts we give are extensions of ourselves, not just our resources, but our very being. The gift without the giver is bare. In fact, gifts are transparent in that the care of the giver is revealed in the gift itself. We must remember this message and not let it get lost in the excitement and bustle of Christmas Day.

O. Henry's Christmas story "The Gift of the Magi" recounts the care of the giver in a lovely way. A poor young couple, so much in love with each other, sacrificed what was most personal to each of them to buy a gift for the other. The woman cut and sold her long hair to buy a watch chain for her husband. He sold his watch to buy decorative combs for his wife.

Not too swift, you might say, and we modern, practical people probably would have checked out what our spouse was doing. The truth of O. Henry's familiar story is the very essence of giving and receiving. We give ourselves to another. The gift we wrap is the sign of that larger gift of love. It is incalculable in cost and unexplainable in purpose. It does not have to be explained. It is understood.

There is often sadness at Christmas as well as joy. There is disappointment sometimes, and, according to social workers, psychiatric caseloads rise. Tinsel and eggnog and jingle-bells are not enough for a day so rich in human aspiration and divine promise.

Our lives are not always tidy and neat. We carry a great deal of baggage with us. Memories are uncomfortable as well as sweet. Guilt and regret are not easily displaced by colorful wrapping paper. A more profound sense of the meaning of giving and receiving is available. It is found in the story of Christmas.

God's gift to us was a person, no tinsel or bright wrapping, but a promise of love. Christians claim to see love itself in the gift of God at Christmas time. The expectation is that we can be transparent to one another in the act of gift giving. That just may turn our lives into new directions of love for others.

GOD IS WITH US

A Gift for Amateurs

Most of my adult life I made my living as a theologian. A theologian is a person who is educated in the history of a religious tradition and who specializes in thinking and talking about God. The word theology, loosely translated from the Greek, could mean "finding reasons for God."

Theologians have played important roles in Western history. Their thinking about God has resulted in the development of Western civilization as we know it. Some theologians, such as Saint Augustine, Saint Thomas, and Martin Luther were so influential that they changed the very way people understood themselves and saw their world. They created intellectual revolutions. They even created new languages to carry their visions.

Theologians were once known for their complicated arguments about one thing or another. There were debates that once may have seemed important but now have lost most of their urgency. The famous discussion of how many angels could dance on the head of a pin is a case in point. Sometimes these theologians were not much help.

Some theologians got us into a lot of trouble as in the terrible times of the Spanish Inquisition. For these theologians, correct belief was a life or death matter. If a person held an incorrect view, it might have resulted in death.

But all through Western Christian history, there has been a kind of nontechnical popular theology. This sometimes frustrated the clergy. This was the theology of the ordinary folks. It was not heavy in doctrine and official teachings of the Church. It grew out of more simple needs and impulses. It was how faith was expressed in ordinary ways all over the Christian world.

Official theologians and clerics were unnerved by this kind of theology. So there developed the idea that there was an "official" point of view with which the majority of Christians could agree. This came to be called orthodoxy. That word means, in Greek, "straight praise" or "correct view." Angles and variations were not acceptable. What a person said about God had to be the party line—straight and true.

When the church was under fire or in troubled times, the religious authorities developed the idea that what was not "straight" was "heresy." This gave a reason for putting the screws (literally) on heretics to compel correct or official religious thought and behavior.

Heresy came in many forms. Usually it was based on

some good ideas, as in the case of the Anabaptists who raised the issue of "believers' baptism" and the Franciscans who thought that the church should exist for the poor. Almost always the heresies came from the simple piety of believers who were more or less untouched by the difficult and sometimes convoluted theological arguments of the clergy.

The festival of Christmas was one such idea. There is universal agreement by scholars that Christmas was a relatively late festival in Christianity. The birth of Jesus is not mentioned in Mark, the oldest document of the four Gospels. The holiday grew out of the ordinary people's need to say something about the touching humanity of their Lord. It eventually replaced an ancient pre-Christian festival called Saturnalia. By the fifth century of the Common Era it was a major element in the way Christians understood themselves.

The unlearned but pious believers took the most familiar human event, the birth of a baby, as their metaphor for the powerful belief that God comes into our human history. They closed the loop on their understanding of religion. They already knew about God as creator and redeemer. But they used the birth stories as the way to confirm their faith in God's humanity.

It was one thing for the theologians to talk about great ideas like the Incarnation (God in human form), the *filioque* clause (the doctrine that the Holy Spirit proceeds from the Father and the Son), and other enlightening concepts. It was something else for the believers to find a way to say that God comes to them in the

GOD IS WITH US

ordinary events of life. These moments do not require extensive explanation, only wonder and praise.

Johannes Brahms may help us here. In his Fourth Symphony in E Minor, no. 4, a lovely and powerful work, he uses almost every convention available to a composer in his time. Much of the work was new and fresh. By the end of the final movement, however, Brahms seems to have reached a climax and to have exhausted invention. Having said all that can be said with the many innovations available to him, he turns unexpectedly to surprise. He resorts to a mighty and sustained blast on the horns. Nothing but a long shout of joy! That is what Christmas is for believers. An uncomplicated celebration of the kind that ordinary folk can understand. It is the shout of joy of the angel chorus, the wonder of the wise, and the song of a new mother to a child.

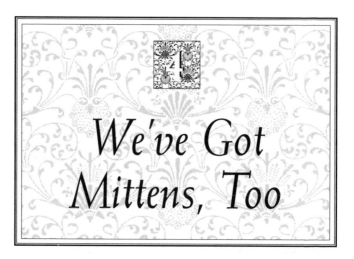

We've Got Mittens, Too

The German soldiers in World War I wore belt buckles with the inscription *Gott mit uns* (God is with us). American doughboys, coping with freezing weather, were not so theological. They were reported to have said, "We've got mittens, too."

This old story reflects the wondrous ambiguity of war. The Germans were proudly asserting that God was with them in the struggle. The Americans, maybe sensing the irony of such claims, turned the motto into a humorous one-liner.

God must be confused in time of war. All sides claim God's active support and blessing. In Bosnia three belligerent sides were fighting under thinly veiled religious mandates. The Croats are Roman Catholic. Most Serbs are Orthodox. The Bosnians are split, the majority of them are either Muslim or Orthodox. Each group carries its cultural memories of warfare and hatred going back to the Islamic invasions of Europe in the four-teenth century and the division of the Christian Church into East and West in the ninth century.

People who cannot let go of the past are doomed to repeat the terrible failures of their ancestors in the future. After four terrible years of bloodshed and unspeakable atrocities against one another, a fragile peace is in place in Bosnia. American troops have been there serving as keepers of the peace along with other NATO partners.

We Americans are often reluctant warriors and peacekeepers. "Home by Christmas" is the powerful hope held out to soldiers in every war. All who have served in the military understand the compelling power of that vision. Whether one is Christian, Jew, or Muslim, the longing for home at religious holidays is intense.

We should be proud of the women and men who stand watch in places such as Bosnia. They have a right to be called peacemakers. Their presence is a reminder to the belligerents that citizens of different religious backgrounds can unite to form a nation of believers. Tolerance and freedom of worship can replace a history of hatred and sectarianism. This is a wonderful model for a world weary of religious strife.

Americans have grown weary of ambiguous interna-tional roles ever since Vietnam. We are apprehensive. Some believe we should not put our troops in harm's way. Others suggest we should send arms but not sol-diers. That, it seems to me, is tantamount to suggesting that the Bosnian war should continue until one faction

emerges bloody but victorious. Then we accept genocide as an acceptable moral position.

So our soldiers are going to be there at the holiday
time. They will make the best of it, and we will see to it
that they have as comfortable a celebration there as it is
possible to arrange. Their presence during our religious
days will serve the wider purpose. It will remind the
Bosnians that nations should stand for something larger
than nostalgia and angry memories.

Christmas and Hanukkah are festivals of hope.
Hanukkah recalls the terrible siege of Jerusalem in the
time of the Maccabees. But it celebrates the rededica-
tion of the Temple, signified by the eight days needed
for the oil to last and the menorah light to burn. When
the light had burned for the eighth day, the cleansing of
the Temple was complete. The Christmas story in Luke
records the angels' song: "Glory to God in the highest
heaven, and on earth peace among those whom he
favors!" (Luke 2:14).

The theme of these great holy days of Christmas is
reconciliation. The world's great religions all look forward to a time when warriors will lay down their
weapons, when spears will be pounded into plow-
blades, and when the lion will lie down with the lamb.
Then peace and the songs of peace will be sung again in
unexpected places.

GOD IS WITH US

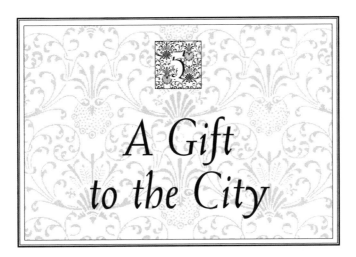

A Gift to the City

*F*ifth Avenue in Manhattan is spectacular during the Christmas season. The stores are crowded with shoppers. Display windows are filled with marvelous animated scenes. The huge lighted tree in Rockefeller Center Plaza takes one's breath away. And everywhere there is excitement and good humor in the sharp pinch of December nights.

In the midst of all that excitement and energy, a quartet of singers are performing Christmas songs. They have no sign introducing a charity. There is no container for contributions. They are just singing seasonal chorales and carols. An appreciative crowd has gathered to listen.

I was curious about who they were and what prompted them to perform this way. The answer was startling in its simplicity. "We don't represent anybody; we're not raising money. We just want to give a

GOD IS WITH US

Christmas gift to the city."

Sometimes it is hard to separate the heady commercialism of the holidays from the directness of gift giving. But this event was like discovering a precious stone in an ore pit. The singers were living out the essence of giving and receiving.

Gift giving and gift receiving are part of the same reflex. They have to do with acknowledging relationships of trust in one's neighbors and friends. This has sacramental significance. It is one way we can affirm our need of one another, a need that must be celebrated once in a while to remind us of our relationships.

In the Christmas story, the gifts that were brought to the baby Jesus were not something an infant especially needed. They were symbols of a far deeper relationship. When the Magi brought gold, frankincense, and myrrh, as the tradition holds, the gifts defined an expectation that the wise men had for the child. Their gifts were worthy of a king who someday would change the shapes of justice and love in the whole world.

The young singers on Fifth Avenue were also defining an expectation. It apparently included the hope that their gift of music would be received for what it was. It was a simple, transparent, and uncomplicated way of saying "thank you" to the city.

Big cities are not often thought of in this light. Have you noticed that the image of the city on television is brutal, bloody, and frightening? Yet there on Fifth Avenue, on a brisk but clear night, with the streets jammed with busy people, four singers were "giving a gift to the city."

GOD IS WITH US

Draw the image larger. Make the city the whole, wide world. Then think of ways that the Christmas message of hope through giving and receiving might make a difference. Christmas is the time of year when we are sure our hope for the world and for one another is not an impossible dream.

Beyond High Technology

*D*elta Air Lines' Christmas card one year revealed Santa Claus and his reindeer in a line of 747s waiting for takeoff. Every traveler who had experienced long delays in similar circumstance was amused.

The anachronism serves to remind us of many wonderful and beautiful things that survive the high-tech world in which we live. The quaint myth of Santa Claus, derived from an historical figure, Saint Nicholas, fits right into our technological landscape.

Some have said that we live in a "post-modern" world. I believe this means that the stories and beliefs that held our society together in a simpler time no longer command the same authority. After all, we have been able to travel in space, put men on the moon, conquer most but not all disease, and even practice genetic engineering.

The Delta Airline card seemed wryly to hint that high technology—wonderful as it is—is not the final expression of human aspiration.

Science is the discipline whereby we determine the way things work in the world. Technology is the way we put scientific knowledge to work for human good. But neither science nor technology ultimately answers the fundamental human questions about the world. Those questions are philosophical and religious questions: What is the meaning of life? Why are we here? Where are we going? What is good? What is valuable? What is true?

These profound issues are frequently obscured under the weight of the superstructure and pace of our lives. Getting from place to place is important. Having a career is important. The technology of travel and communication and career often deflect serious reflection about more substantial human issues.

Religious seasons of the year can be times of increased anxiety and depression. These are the seasons when basic human questions are pushed into consciousness. They are the times when deferred dreams and disappointments have to be dealt with. All our technology and knowledge seems not to be so helpful. Right there, in the midst of the long line of 747s, sits Santa and the reindeer.

Thomas Hardy was a sophisticated, somewhat cynical novelist and poet in England early in this century. In one of his most touching poems, "The Oxen," he recalled the tradition that held that farm animals knelt in their stalls at midnight on Christmas Eve. The animals were rehearsing the first Christmas in a stable. This sweet and gentle tradition was remembered by children who would leave food for the farm animals on Christmas Eve.

Christmas Eve, and twelve of the clock.
  'Now they are all on their knees,'
An elder said as we sat in a flock
  By the embers in hearthside ease.

We pictured the meek mild creatures where
  They dwelt in their strawy pen,
Nor did it occur to one of us there
  To doubt they were kneeling then.

So fair a fancy few would weave
  In these years! Yet, I feel,
If someone said on Christmas Eve,
  'Come; see the oxen kneel,

'In the lonely barton by yonder coomb
  Our childhood used to know,'
I should go with him in the gloom,
  Hoping it might be so.

The persistence of these sweet reminders of simpler times is not an illustration of ignorance or cultural deprivation. It is rather the persistence of the human questions about the meaning of life. The Christmas stories are not untrue. They are too true to be told in the languages of high technology. They can only be expressed where they are available to us in lovely, simple, childlike ways.

The words associated with Christmas are words such as joy, peace, love, friendship, charity, glory, mercy, truth, birth. These are the words that describe our humanity. The Christmas stories embody these words.

The contours of the stories form the words into meaningful language. The gift from a parent to a child or a child to sibling or a stranger to a stranger describes without scientific or technological explanation what it means to be human.

We are at our best or our worst at times like these. At Christmas we come close to believing that the world is really put together the way love intends.

At Christmastime, when you find yourself sitting in a plane on a busy airport runway, look out the window. It just may be that the Christ Child, the Magi, the shepherds, or the angel Gabriel are waiting also. I'm going to look, like Hardy, "hoping it might be so."

Conserving Christmas

At the J. Paul Getty Museum in Malibu, California, one will find one of the finest art collections in the world. Getty, a fabulously successful oil developer, left his estate to a foundation that continues his work of gathering extraordinary art for his museum. The museum is particularly interested in Greek and Roman antiquities and in the riches of Medieval European art.

Behind the scenes at the Getty Museum is a highly skilled group of workers who look after the collection and who are called conservators. These people use the latest scientific instruments to verify authenticity and to help them in the work of caring for ancient but some-times damaged art. They use X-rays, infrared spectro-graphs, and carbon dating in their work. They study other works from comparable periods. They develop computer models to help them plan for conservation.

A valuable work of art may arrive at the museum in

many pieces. Statuary and vases have been damaged over the centuries. The puzzle of analyzing and assembling the art is the work of the laboratories at the museum.

Much of what the conservators do is determining what other people have done earlier to the work. I saw a lovely Roman copy of a Greek Leda and the Swan being studied in the lab. It had been worked over several times in history, including a coat or two of shellac and major revisions in the statue itself. Sometimes clothing would be altered or added to certain parts of the anatomy to suit the sensibilities of a particular generation.

These treatments of the art were at the hands of "restorers," the name used to describe artists who "restore" an ancient and damaged work to its so-called "original" state. Frequently as not the "restorers" had their own ideas of what Greek or Roman art ought to be. So they restored the work to their own ideal of Greek or Roman art rather than letting the art speak for itself. The result is that much ancient art has been lost in the hands of those who sought to improve it.

At the Getty Museum and in other centers today, the workers in the laboratories think of themselves as "conservators," conserving the art in its own history. This will include even the several stages of restoration. The conservator tries not to impose some modern theory of ancient beauty on a work of art, but rather lets the art speak for itself. The history is part of the art object. This research may also save us from fakes that flood the art marketplace.

So the laboratory workers are busy making it possible for us to appreciate the beauty of other ages. They also help us understand the problematic history of art as these wonderful objects come to us in the late 20th century.

At Christmastime it may be helpful to contemplate the difference between "restoration" and "conservation." The risk of restoration is that we may impose on an art object or a religious event our own personal taste and views as to the appropriateness of the event. Conservation, on the other hand, suggests that what we have received is not only the original event, but the fullness of the history of the event. Who has touched it? What has it meant to other generations of witnesses? What can we learn from them?

Christmas is an event for "conservators." Its meanings are enriched by everyone who is touched by it or touches it in some way. We are not particularly helped by knowing the detail of the original celebration. The annual celebration, involving our own family and friends, is the real thing.

Each year we try to find a way to take off the old shellac, grown yellow with age, and present a fresh and lively face to the world that is hungry for beauty.

Guess Who's Coming!

A pastor opened the children's sermon one Sunday in Advent by asking the youngsters, "Advent means 'coming'! Who's coming?" With one voice they chorused, "Santa Claus!"

Of course the traditional expectation is the coming of Christ. Advent, in churches that follow liturgical practice, begins the fourth Sunday preceding Christmas Day. During that season the hymns and prayers of the church remind believers of the longing of Israel for the Messiah and the hope that the coming of the Messiah was imminent.

One does not expect pre-schoolers to be sophisticated about the liturgical year, but then many of their parents have the same response. We live in a period when many of the religious traditions of our various communities have been replaced by a "post-religious" spirit.

Santa Claus is a remarkable example of this phenomenon. He is a jolly fellow, whose mythical abode at the North Pole with its shop of elves making toys for boys and girls is familiar to all. His mode of transportation is a sleigh with reindeer, and he enters homes on Christmas Eve by descending through the chimneys.

Now I don't want to knock Santa Claus. The Santa tradition is a sweet and gentle thing and full of symbolism for all of us. But for post-modern folk who think some religious traditions are quaint or pre-scientific, apparently the Santa Claus tradition has fewer problems! Reindeer sky-diving, an overweight old man entering a house via the chimney, elves working at the North Pole? Give me a break!

Even though we are modern, we live with many stories and myths. The loss of real religious faith will require new and more accommodating fictions. Gabriel Vahanian once remarked that each revival of religious faith seems to be a revival of less and less. It also seems to come fascinated with rites and stories from exotic religious traditions. For most modernity, exotic stories and traditions are all right if they come from a non-Christian context.

The power and beauty of the Christmas story lies in its simplicity and directness. The first Christians were astonished to discover that the Messiah they had long expected came to them in a most surprising but believable way. He came as a baby born to a peasant family in an unlikely corner of the world.

Most of us are conditioned to expect fireworks and large stages for really serious moments. The pyrotechnic displays at the baseball park when someone hits a home run are more spectacular than the birth of a child in a barn in a remote countryside.

But every mother and father know the deep joy of childbirth. They know the vastness of their hope for their newborn child. For them it is a cosmic event, a glorious moment that opens their eyes to the possibilities of life and history and love.

Advent is the time when Christians contemplate the layers of meaning that come at Christmastime. Who is coming? That is the question that everyone must answer for himself or herself. Is it Santa with his gentle and jolly good humor and gifts for deserving boys and girls? I hope Santa comes to our house.

More importantly, I hope for the coming of the Christ Child. For his coming promises the hope for joy and love and justice and family strength and a world made new.

Handling Expectations

*C*hristmas is a time of extraordinary expectation. Religiously it is the celebration of the coming of the promised Messiah, the one who would liberate humankind from fear and sin and suffering. But the expectation is often overwhelmed by disappointment. Just as expectation and joy are built into the celebration, so also can disappointment be programmed.

Gift giving can become mixed up with the ego of the gift giver. The frenzy of giving sometimes overtakes the purpose of giving, and confusion results. The zany practice of exchanging gifts after the holiday is an example of the misunderstanding we create. What ought to be a ceremony of love, the giving and receiving of symbols of our care for one another, frequently can become a time of calculated and pretentious exchange of merchandise. Thoughtful persons can be excused of being a bit sad and wistful at times like that.

But more likely the cause of holiday sadness is the recollection of the richness of the circles of love that are a family's history. Moments like Christmas are the times of definition of who we are as children and parents and brothers and sisters. For those whose lives have taken turns away from that history, the richness and texture of memory persists. As Christmas nears, only the hard-hearted and cynical will fail to feel some pang of nostalgia for innocence lost.

If one longs to return to the bosom of the family but cannot, then holiday sadness will prevail. If one won't return because of some real or imagined lack of trust, then holiday sadness will persist. And for some, stricken with illness or loss of job, the sheer pain of separation from participation in the expectations of the holiday will be reason for despair.

The promise of the Christmas holiday, the coming of the Messiah, is itself the occasion for putting aside all loneliness, suffering, and anxiety. Out of darkness comes the light of freedom and the strength to face every trial.

So here is a good question: Can we really handle too much expectation? Isn't it better to keep our sights low and our longings within reasonable goals? Christmas, a celebration of light, suggests that the religious community has riches it even does not fully understand. The hope that is celebrated in the holidays still drives us to new levels of faithfulness to our own histories and our own aspirations. The underside of the holiday—with the sense of despair that seems to come with the celebration—reminds us both that we are human and that we are all in need of hope.

Ideologues and Christmas

Great religious holidays recall unexpected and surprising events. This sense of unexpectedness lingers in the celebrations. The lighting of candles reminds us of the unexpected light that shines in the darkness. The Christmas story reminds us that God chooses the very least and humble in the world to be the bearer of the good news. These are unusual events.

The Christmas festival is a reminder that being religious means keeping one's eyes and ears open to the unexpected. Historical religions, such as Judaism and Christianity, are full of such reminders that God speaks through events. The prophets of Israel had a lot to say about people who refused to hear what God was saying in those events. Jesus was also frustrated by his friends who failed often to understand what his message was all about.

Most of us are restless with the idea that we can be

surprised by religious insights. We like our religion "well done." We are comfortable with the familiar and the rehearsed. Our ideas about religion are important to us, and we become anxious when those ideas are challenged.

Frequently the prophets and Jesus had to remind their listeners that they were introducing new ways of looking at God's way with the world. "You have heard that it was said to those of ancient times . . ., But I say to you . . . " is a frequent introduction to a teaching of Jesus. It is hard to give up comfortable ideas and dependable ways of organizing one's world. Clarence Day's father in his novel *Life with Father* was said to address God in prayer as if he were a guest in a mismanaged hotel.

The person who loves an idea about something more than the reality itself is an "ideologue." The word comes from the Greek roots for "idea" and "structure." An ideologue may be a person who loves "religion" but can't get along with people. An ideologue may be a person who feels strongly about democracy, but doesn't trust the electorate. An ideologue may be more concerned for a dogmatic view even though events have changed. An ideologue is a person whose mind is made up and does not want to be confused by facts.

There is a difference between holding strong beliefs and being an ideologue. Ideologues test reality by their ideas. Others test their ideas by reality. In religion and in politics, ideologues have special problems. They have to find others who agree with them in their strongly held ideas. This makes for some difficulty because communities by nature are somewhat ambiguous. There are other views and ideas to be taken into account. In an open community, the vigorous exchange of ideas is considered necessary. In an ideological organization, differing views are frequently considered to be "dissent" or "heresy."

The holiday season is a good time to test one's tolerance for freshness and the unexpected in public and religious life. Just how much new insight can we tolerate in ordering our lives? Maybe that is why Christmas is such an important holiday for modern folk. Christmas is more than a time for family reunion and good cheer. It is a reminder of the power of new beginnings, fresh insight, and a chance to look at the world with new eyes. It is no time for ideologues.

In the darkness of midwinter, Christ comes to bring light and healing.

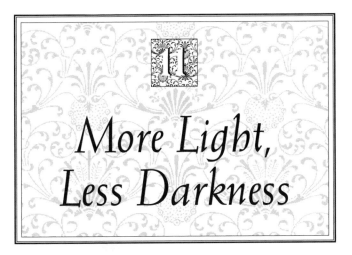

More Light, Less Darkness

Christmas comes at the darkest time of the year. At least this is so for people in the Northern Hemisphere where the holiday began. The winter solstice occurs on or about December 21. On that magic day we start adding minutes to daylight instead of subtracting them.

No one knows the actual birthdate of Jesus. It is not uncommon for birthdays to be celebrated on convenient dates. Queen Elizabeth II of Great Britain officially celebrates her birthday in sunny June although she was born in rainy April. Wet parades are not much fun. Why was the "bleak midwinter" chosen as the appropriate time to remember the birth of Jesus? Why not bright summer or flowering spring?

Darkness suggests the human moods of anxiety and fear. In its more benign forms it may be experienced by people in the northernmost regions as seasonal affective disorder or SAD. It is cabin fever. Darkness is also a frightening metaphor for the feeling of a world gone awry, without hope and joy.

How shall we cope with the darkness of violence? Dark streets are not safe in many cities. We experience the shock of random killings by otherwise ordinary people. Persons are losing jobs in industries that we never thought would have layoffs. Surely to many of us this is a time of darkness.

No other season more fully expresses the mood of dread than the darkness of winter. Longing for sunlight is a metaphor for hope. Hanukkah is the "festival of lights," and biblical language is full of the metaphors of light. The prophet Isaiah promised that the expected Messiah would be his people's "everlasting light." So it was natural for Jews to think that the coming of the Messiah would be celebrated with light and brightness. The metaphor is complete. In the darkness of midwinter, Christ comes to bring light and healing. After Christmas the days become longer and warmer and darkness and dread retreat.

Christmas and Hanukkah remind us that darkness is not this world's permanent state. Christmas is the story of the victory of Light over darkness. The story behind Hanukkah is the memory that when the people were in deep crisis there was light enough. Christmas and Hanukkah come in the darkest time of the year to tell us that light will win.

"The people who sat in darkness
    have seen a great light,
    and for those who sat in the
      region and shadow of death
light has dawned" (Matt. 4:16).

People who experience the reality of these great celebrations are touched by the beauty of the traditions, the music, the happy family gatherings, and the loveliness of the stories. But the purpose of all religious celebrations is more profound that even these things. The intention is to move the world toward more light and less darkness. The spirit of hope that arises in these holiday moments reminds us of the need to be what the early Christians called "children of light."

Early Christians had taken on the metaphor of light to become agents of change in the world. They sought righteousness and justice. They cast their light into the dark corners of prejudice and hate and inhumanity. These believers gave hope to those who still lived in darkness. They visited the widows and orphans, the sick and those cast out and in prison. They made their communities places of hope in a brighter future. They taught all women and men to trust in each other as children of the Light.

As we observe these days, it is a good thing to think about these ancient celebrations of Christmas and Hanukkah and how they may change lives. Other solutions are not working.

The coming of the Christ Child is the confirmation of hope that God is at work in the world.

Nostalgia and Hope

*T*he Romans had a god named Janus who had two faces. He could look backward and forward at the same time. He is remembered in the name of the first month of the year—January.

Christmas is a special time for many because it is the festival of hope that is anchored in the past. In a profound way Christmas looks in two directions. For believers, the coming of the Christ Child was an event promised for centuries in the prophecies of Israel. For a world desperate for meaning, the coming was the announcement of a new future.

It is important that we recognize the past—where we have been. But it is equally important that we look to the future—where we want to be heading. Living in the present requires an awareness of the tension between the two times.

These sentiments are inextricably wrapped up in the

lovely carols of Christmas. Jesus is announced as the promised messiah of Israel and great joy greets the announcement. But the promise of the future takes a startlingly new form. The messiah comes in the shape of an innocent and helpless baby. History and innocence intersect in shaping a powerful moment of Christian belief.

We experience something of the same cycle in our own celebrations of Christmas. For many it is a time of nostalgia, rich in memories of loved ones gathering in family settings, remembering the past and being touched by all sorts of signs of love.

Because of the powerful pull of memory, Christmas may also be a time of remorse and sadness. It may be a time of regret for failed gestures of reconciliation. It is hoped that Christmas is a time of new beginnings. The birth of the Christ Child was such a time in history.

The Gospel writers and the later traditions of the first Christmas remind us that the healing of the past in the present is a fragile process. The hope that lies in the Christmas story is not the discovery of some sort of superman who will dramatically change the course of events.

God enters into our personal histories as a sign of hope. There is nothing in the world more hopeful than a baby. At the same time there is nothing more helpless. The hope of a world made new is inextricably tied to our own intention to care for the helpless. Movement toward reconciliation and meaning in our lives is measured in an infant's movements. Christmas is the time of great joy because the promise of a world made new in the intentions of God is assured. Persons must now measure their own lives by the degree of their own caring for the world.

If you look behind the secular furniture of Christmas you can glimpse the meaning of the event. The giving of gifts is the descriptive act of how a world is made new in hope. Ordinary human relationships are directed toward those we love and those who are unnamed neighbors. Food baskets are symbols of our need to share ourselves with those who have need of us. The family gatherings are recapitulations of the ancient mystery of time past and time forward.

Nostalgia is healthy when it is tied to future hopefulness. It becomes dangerous when it is nursed by resentment and disappointment about the past. For Christian believers, the coming of the Christ Child is the confirmation of hope that God is at work in the world. Christmas is a time when it may be possible for us to shuck off the burdensome disappointments of our own histories and say with the carol, "Let every heart prepare him room."

The Festival of Hope

Many post-modern folk are wary of religion. They may recall some touching early memory of Christmas past, but they are profoundly skeptical of their own need for Christmas. Such wistfulness seems almost religious in these days. There is a profound cynicism loose in our time and it is out of fashion to be hopeful. But hope defines who we are, and wistfulness is a luxury we cannot bear.

A person is what a person trusts. Hope is commitment to the future as a livable time. Hope is the confidence one has in the ultimate triumph of good. Hope is the measure of our willingness to risk self-interest for some larger purpose.

Christmas is the season of hope. The stories of Christmas are filled with this forward look. Hope drove Mary and Joseph to find a place of security for the birth of Jesus. Hope brought the shepherds to the stall. Hope drove the Magi at great risk to worship the Child. Hope made the Gospel writers recall the passionate words of Isaiah that the one who comes will be called Immanuel, that is, "God is with us!"

All about us we see evidence of hopelessness. Terrible and interminable regional wars give no reason for careless innocence. Disappointment in governments' covert activities does not lend itself to hope. The rising gaps between the poor and the rich around the world are not reassuring.

Our fear of nuclear disaster paralyzes us. Aimlessness is a by-product of hopelessness. The "good news" of hopelessness is "everyone for him- or herself." Consumption, privatism, and instant gratification seem to be the accepted antidotes to hopelessness.

In such times as these, Christmas becomes a more urgent season of hope. The story of Christmas is the story of God's way of giving us the good news. That good news is that our best dreams for the world are coming true.

This took place in the most humble surroundings in an obscure corner of the world. We would not have understood this mystery so well had the events been more spectacular. Every parent can relate to the joy of a birth and the surge of hope that new life brings. So God chose understandable ways to declare the reign of love.

Samuel Miller, late dean of the Harvard Divinity School, once wrote these words: "God speaks to us about eternity in terms of the little events of time." A birth, a simple act of love, a selfless act of trust in another person, breaking bread together, feeding the hungry, healing the sick—all these are little events in time that make visible the wider purposes of God.

It may seem crazy to think that simple love and care for justice can overcome the terrible and fearful shapes of our world. But that is the Christmas message. It's worth a try.

The Gifts Beyond Value

The Christmas story has not changed. It is the same story with its power to challenge the imagination. But during times of recession there is a general anxiety abroad in the land. Retail merchants have sleepless nights as the annual spending for gifts is curtailed, and we utter "Christmas is going to be different this year."

Christmas can be different for other reasons as well. The major powers have backed off after almost half a century of Cold War. We have made some progress in settling long standing arguments in Ireland, the Holy Land, and Bosnia. There is new hope for finding cures to grim reapers of human life such as AIDS and cancer.

These are all gifts beyond imagining a few years ago. Just as in the Christmas story the Magi from the East brought gifts to the Christ Child, we may think of these great social and political changes as gifts surpassing a seasonal commercial frenzy.

Christmas is the most earthy of the Christian religious observances. In Christianity, God takes on the form of a human person. This is a remarkable and outrageous assertion—foolish and scandalous, according to Paul of Tarsus.

The point of this assertion of faith is not to suggest some magic or extra-terrestrial happening. This is not pyrotechnics. It is not like the northern lights or sunspots. It is the declaration that God enters the world in decisive ways to tell us human beings what the big picture is all about.

The joy of giving and receiving gifts is a treasured family experience. But the dependence on spending may have obscured other gifts for which we can be grateful and other persons who need our love. So, this year our list should include the poor, the hungry, the jobless, the homeless, the widows and orphans, those who suffer from physical disabilities, and those for whom the light of Christmas is felt as the pain of loss.

The Christmas story is the claim that the world's reason for being is love. Not the sentimental kind favored in soap operas. But the love once described by a wise commentator as "love with its eyes open." So, maybe, just maybe, we will be closer to the spirit of Christmas this year than we have been for some time. Christmas really belongs to all those people in our world who long for love and peace and hope.

✣

GOD IS WITH US

The Gift of Self

T he tradition of giving and receiving gifts at
Christmastime has its roots in the story of the Magi and
the Christ Child. The so-called "wise men" from the
East followed the star and presented dramatic and ironic
gifts to the babe in the manger, so the story goes.

The gifts were indeed ironic and symbolic. The gold
represented kingship, frankincense represented divinity,
and myrrh was a burial ointment. The gifts and the visit
of the Magi were a prefiguration of the suffering of Jesus
as well as a salute to his birth.

Gift giving is universal in human cultures. It is one
way that people celebrate their relationship to one
another. Gifts of enjoyment and entertainment are fun
to receive. It is also fun, sometimes, to get a utilitarian
gift, like a tie or a steam iron. Giving gifts, then, is a
way we define our roles and obligations each to the
other. But the true spirit of Christmas lies behind the

gift. This is the gift that counts.

The gift that changes lives and makes for new community is the gift of self. That is why it is so important for people to put themselves at risk in giving. Working in the social service programs as a volunteer is a gift of great value. Helping as a volunteer in a hospital or working with people in a hospice are expressions of the gift of self.

Christina Rossetti, the Victorian poet, expressed it well in a poem. One of the stanzas raises the question about appropriateness of gifts.

> What can I give Him,
> poor as I am?
> If I were a shepherd
> I would bring a lamb,
> If I were a Wise Man
> I would do my part,—
> Yet what can I give Him,
> Give my heart.

The gift of oneself is the appropriate gift at Christmas. The Christmas story suggests that God gave himself to the world in the form of the babe of Bethlehem. To give oneself to others—parents, children, neighbors, those in need of us—is the gift that ultimately gives Christmas its magic and its power.

Look over your gift list. Simplify it by imagining the gift of self.

16

The Gift of Vulnerability

Christmas Eve is a magical time. It is a time of remembrance and of hope. It is a time when families are closer together than they may be all year. It is a time when persons make an effort to be in touch with one another. Christmas Eve is the moment when the Christian world takes a big breath and contemplates the reasons for things.

Christmas Eve is a time for family rituals. When our children were young, we left a cup of hot chocolate on the hearth for Santa Claus. In the morning the children looked to see if Santa had in fact arrived and enjoyed the warm drink. Even now as adults our children insist on the ritual.

The popular candlelight services on Christmas Eve have this magical quality. The worshipers are like the Magi and the shepherds, bringing gifts of love to the stable. There is an air of expectancy and joy in the place and feelings of good will in the greetings of friends.

People have needs all year around, but somehow at Christmas everyone is more sensitive to those needs than normally. Our caring reflexes are quicker at Christmas. We say nice things to strangers. We visit neighbors we haven't seen all year. We may not be especially "religious" persons, but we get into the spirit of things during this religious season.

The moods of Christmas Eve are a mixture of surprise and assurance. The Christmas story itself is one of surprises. The "expected" Messiah was looked for as someone who would arrive in majesty and power, probably a military hero, at least a prominent politician.

But God, maybe with a suggestion of a sense of humor, sent his messenger in the form of a baby. That was surprise enough! A baby is among the most vulnerable beings in the world. How is it that the all-powerful God, the Infinite Creator of the universe, would send the most finite of beings, a baby, as a sign of God's love for the world?

The giving and receiving of gifts is part of the theme of surprise and joy. The excitement of the unexpected yet expected is a recapitulation of the first Christmas event. We are the Magi to one another in the giving of gifts. We are shepherds looking in amazement at the signs of joy.

There is a profound reassurance in the Christmas event. In the story, God tells his people that love has something to do with vulnerability. Love is putting one's self in one's neighbor's need. Love is risking one's life for another. Love is taking a chance on some one else's trust. Love is forgiving the insults and slights to oneself. Love is putting up with people who are not lovable. In short, love is becoming vulnerable to the other's needs.

When you think of it, vulnerability is a good definition of love in the family or the extended family. In the bosom of the family all the permutations of love are tested and refined. In a loving family, the strength of love is a cause for celebration. Christmas is the festival of sharing love in ways that continually surprise us and reassure us.

There is another tradition about Christmas. It is the memory of hate and fear that surrounded the birth of the Christ Child. King Herod, warned about the birth of a political messiah, determined to kill all the male babies in the land. We have seen similar atrocities in recent years. Christmas Eve is a time to contemplate the cost of love. Sometimes in our own families we have to take risks to heal the pain of separation. But also in the community and the world, Christmas is a time for healing and rebinding the ties of love.

The cost of love is measured by the risks involved. The price of love is another matter. In a world that has put monetary value on almost everything, the one priceless gift is love that makes no claims in return. In a world that seems to have few reasons for hope, the gift of love at Christmas is "the hope of the world."

It may be risky to act on that vision. But that's really what Christmas is all about.

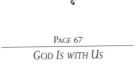

The Hard Side of Christmas

Christmas is a time of gentleness and caring. It is a time for good feeling to neighbors and good cheer to strangers. The songs are sweet and the spirit is merry. Like all holidays, it is a time for celebration of what is humanly important to us.

But the context of the first Christmas was not so comfortable. The recounting of the events surrounding the first Christmas does provide a slight chill of apprehension. The story began with a journey to a distant city by a woman and her husband, the woman in late pregnancy. No accommodations were available. The woman delivered in a stable. Fearful because of rumors that the king wanted to destroy the child, the couple escaped by darkness into another country. The king, angered at the escape, ordered all male children under the age of two to be destroyed. Merry Christmas!

There is a tendency in religious practice to clean things

up a bit. That makes the ugly events more tolerable. The cross becomes jewelry. Imagine the electric chair on a golden chain to get the force of that irony. The story of Christmas has been focused on the beauty of the birth and the angelic chorus and the visits by shepherds and Magi.

But this has the result of hiding the hard reality of the tradition. The hard side is the fact that not everyone welcomes love as the rule in human relations. Not everyone is overjoyed at the thought that social relations would now be different, that the poor would have a place in the sun. Not everyone feels comfortable with justice as the norm of human society.

The news of Christmas is still good news. Beyond the cruelty and self-interest and alienation of this world, there is the hope that a new life is possible. Through contemplation of the Christmas event we may yet understand God's intentions for the human family. This is the deeper joy of the holiday. It is good news for those who have given up on joy.

A Christmas hymn by James Montgomery suggests the purpose of the Christmas Child:

He comes to break oppression, to set the
captive free;
to take away transgression, and rule in equity.
He comes with succor speedy to those who
suffer wrong;
to help the poor and needy, and bid the weak
be strong.

We sing this but may not hear what we sing. Joy at Christmas is only possible if the songs are sung . . . and understood.

The Intersection of Hopes and Fears

Christmas Eve is the sum of the thousand ways that people touch one another. It is as close as we will get to Bethlehem. "The hopes and fears of all the years are met in thee tonight," said Phillips Brooks about Christmas in Bethlehem in his famous hymn.

Tradition holds that the first Christmas Eve was a time of irony and high drama. There were great expectations. The long-promised Messiah had arrived but in an improbable way. Restless folk in Israel looked for a military hero. But he came as a helpless baby, the exact opposite of conventional expectation.

One would have thought that the parents of this special child would have been welcomed in some comfortable inn. They were lucky to find a place in the stable behind the inn. There the most interesting and influential person in all history was born with the farm animals as witnesses.

GOD IS WITH US

A fearful king heard rumors of the birth. Like all tyrants, Herod was unsure of his power. So fearful was he that he ordered his soldiers to seek out the child and murder him in the horrible efficiency of totalitarians. Herod's troops slaughtered thousands of infants.

The first Christmas Eve was a time of mixed emotions. Fear, as well as joy. We know the joy as expressed by the angelic chorus. We read of the reverence of the shepherds who were directed to the scene by the angels. Later on, when the Magi came to pay homage, we sense the solemnity of these wise men as they presented their gifts.

So Christmas is a time of reflection on the complexity of life. Like the first Christmas, this year it will be a time of hope and expectancy, mixed with joy and maybe some fear. Yet Christmastime provides confidence in the future in spite of the signs that make confidence fragile. The Christmas season is the most human of holidays, and Christmas Eve is its intersection of hope and fear. May it be memorable for you.

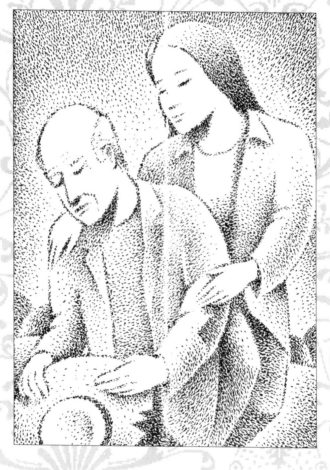

The love and care that binds families together is part of the fabric of religious meaning.

The Response to Indifference

We can use a good dose of Christmas this year. Christmas is the holiday that focuses on the theme of all the great religions: Those without food or shelter or rights or privilege have a claim on those who do have those things.

Lately, in our political rhetoric, we appear to be turning our backs on the poor, the "strangers within the gates" (immigrants), widows, and orphans. At this time in our history, we seem to be inventing what might be called a politics of indifference.

The Christmas story is the response to indifference. It centers on the way in which God comes into the world precisely for those left over and left out. The theme is God's care for those who have been without care. Why else would the story be framed in the fragile forms of helplessness—young parents fleeing from political violence, an infant born in a stable and placed in an animal's feeding trough and visited by the herdsmen who sense the presence of hope?

Christmas does bring out reflexes of compassion that are inherent in the holiday. Community organizations prepare food baskets for the poor and toys for the children who otherwise would have no gifts. Many of us find time to work in shelters, serving in soup kitchens. This authentic response to the community's need is in the great tradition of Christmas gift giving.

The profound rituals of family gatherings at this season are also part of the legacy of Christmas as a time of caregiving. The deep longing for the hearths of home at Christmas is reason enough to be thankful for the holiday. The love and care that binds families together is part of the fabric of religious meaning.

The festival of Christmas shares with Judaism and Islam and other great religions the compelling idea that our definitions of family need always to be enlarged. Charity has come to be understood in optional and bureaucratic terms in recent times. Thus we can experiment with indifference as a political policy. In its earliest forms, however, the word "charity" had more wallop.

Charity, in bygone years, had to do with the responsibility of human beings reaching out to neighbors in their need. This inevitably required the widening of the definition of neighbor. A neighbor was not only someone who lived next door, but also persons in need wherever they were. Imagination was added to caregiving.

The great religious heroes and saints are caregivers. In fact, one might say that the definition of a saint is a person who has enlarged our definition of who is our family. Martin Luther King, Jr. showed us how older definitions of family could be replaced by the religious impulse of justice. Mother Teresa of Calcutta extends our definition to the care of those on the outer fringes of hopelessness. Saint Francis of Assisi eventually included all living things in his family.

When you sing the familiar hymns and carols of Christmas you may sense this solidarity of the human family in the confident joy of the music. Encourage that feeling. It is an important part of the Christmas spirit.

❦

A Theology of Christmas

Christmas is the holiday for families. Some holidays remember battles. Some recall the anniversaries of famous events in history. Others remind us of the great leaders of our nation. But Christmas has become the day for families.

Christmas is celebrated widely as a secular holiday. Next to the celebration of Easter for Christians and Yom Kippur for Jews, it is probably the most theological of all special days. After all, the history of Christmas is the telling of the Christians' belief in the coming of the Messiah.

That profound religious affirmation is remembered by faithful folk and honored in church services. But for most people Christmas is an opportunity to focus for a time on the joys and delights of being with the family. "I'll be home for Christmas," says a popular song of 1943.

Some Scrooge-like types complain that the holiday has lost its way. Every once in awhile you will hear someone suggest that it is time to "put Christ back into Christmas." As they used to say in seminary, "That'll preach!"

But when one looks deeply into the dynamics of Christmas, one finds an understanding about life and human relationships that is very near what theologians suggest God intended when he sent the Christ Child into our world.

The theological language about Christmas uses words like incarnation and messiah and hope. These words mean rather simple ideas. The Incarnation suggests that the most cosmic event—the coming of God into the world—has taken place in the most simple and natural event imaginable, the birth of a child. The child is declared to be the Messiah, the messenger of the rule of God in human events. The message is hope that even in the worst of times the best of things can happen to people who look for strength in one another.

Unwrap the gift of Christmas from its theological language and you have the family Christmas celebration. The family is the metaphor for God's intention for the world. Bound each to the other by flesh and by love and nurtured in the hope that sustains its members through crisis, the family is drawn together in this profoundly religious way. But sometimes it is not described as religious–it only feels important and necessary and renewing.

A great Swiss theologian of recent times once noted that "God looks out at us from eternity with a human face." That is the meaning of Incarnation. The language of Christmas theology says "The Word was made flesh." The language of religion becomes visible and real in the context of human relationships. At Christmas we all become aware of that in varying degrees of intensity.

The family traditions at Christmas are as religiously profound as whatever is taking place in the church sanctuary. Gifts are signs of continuing love and mutual responsibility for one another. The Christmas meal is a kind of sacrament as surely as a priestly offering. The personal memories of joy and, yes, even sadness, are the stuff of our character.

And, as confident as we are of the bonds of family, in some ways we are always reminded at Christmas that our families are models for the whole human family. The seasonal care we express for our neighbors' needs is a hint of the deep religious significance of the Christian message. The great Christmas hymn is a hymn of joy to the world.

Think about some of these things as we come to Christmas. And may the day be filled with family love and a widening circle of care for the whole world's family. That's what theology is about anyway.

God Is with Us

The Surprises of Christmas

Most of us have memories of holidays that were special even beyond the normal expectations of the day. It may have been that a long-lost relative appeared to remind everyone of the pull of love over alienation. Or one of the youngsters present revealed a depth of spirit or character that surprises all the skeptical aunts and uncles. At some point in family histories, children do become adults.

Out of the perfectly ordinary and normally scripted event, sometimes memorable things happen. It might be a sudden experience of wonder and amazement at the sheer joy of a holiday. In spite of our attempts to contain our emotions, we may even break into tears at the beauty of ordinariness.

At times like that we experience the strong suggestion that the stories we have told one another about belief and faith are in fact true.

The extraordinary jumps out at us from the ordinary. John Steinbeck wrote about this in his novel *The Winter of Our Discontent*. The hero is an old-line aristocratic New Englander now down in his luck. He is employed as a grocery clerk by a recent Italian immigrant. One day they have an argument, and the aristocrat insults the immigrant by impugning his humble background. Murullo scoffs at his employee's comment that his family had been in the town for three hundred years. With great pride and grace, the immigrant traces his ancestry back two thousand years or more in Italy. Shaken by shame and remorse, the hero says, "If I have missed this, what else have I failed to see?"

Christmas celebrations are often big productions with bell, book, and candle. We can easily overlook the humble setting of the first Christmas. It was about as ordinary as is possible to imagine. A corner of a stable in a remote area of a tiny, occupied country far away from the highways of commerce or power was the setting. Christians believe that the story's setting has a great deal to do with the meaning of Christmas itself.

We need to have an inner sense of expectancy to discern what is going on in our world. It is not enough to be confident that ordinary events without meaning are taking place. Some extraordinary things just might be going on in our neighborhoods and we take no notice. If we miss this, what else have we failed to see?

One of the marvelous lines from the Book of Job reveals his discovery of the wider and deeper meanings to otherwise ordinary if terrible events. Repentance from the arrogance of self-centeredness leads Job to

GOD IS WITH US

utter one of the most noble and insightful lines in our tradition. "I had heard of you by the hearing of the ear, but now my eye sees you" (Job 42:5).

Christmas approached with such expectancy will not disappoint us.

*Who is
my neighbor?*

Christmas and the Uses of Imagination

*H*ave you heard this one?

A Pacific cruise ship was passing a small group of desert islands. One passenger pointed excitedly to a ragged, bearded man who was running up and down, waving wildly.

"Who on earth is that?" the passenger asked the captain.

"Dunno," the captain replied. "But he enjoys our visits. He waves and sometimes screams like that every time we pass this way."

An amusing joke, but a serious parable of our times also.

It is difficult for people in stress or need to get attention. Most of us have a reluctance to get involved with such persons. At Christmas we will put a coin in a Salvation Army bucket but that can be done without even recognizing need. Like the sea captain in the story, many of us lack the imagination to respond to need when it presents itself. An organized and well-ordered life is no small achievement, and we are reluctant to have it interrupted.

The Christmas story is above all a story of an interrupted life. Mary and Joseph found it difficult to locate a place for the young woman to deliver her baby. They were on their way to enroll for payment of taxes and later had to flee to a foreign land to escape the hatred of the monarch.

The details of the Christmas story are now so familiar that it takes an act of imagination to put oneself in the story. We are like the sea captain who has grown so used to seeing the desperation of the man on the desert island that he thinks he is witnessing greetings. What the captain lacks is that important human gift, the gift of imagination.

Imagination provides the wider landscapes of experience so that the forms of beauty and understanding may be discerned.

Putting ourselves in another person's situation by imagination is the first step in being connected to the world. Imagining what it is like to suffer loss or pain or injustice is to begin to correct the causes of human suffering in the world.

The ethical imagination has been central to all the great religions. The moral act of putting oneself in the place of another to understand and to feel that person's need is universal. The teachings of Jesus in the New Testament are especially direct. Jesus called on people to put themselves at risk with and for others.

In one of his stories, Jesus described a man beaten and left for dead beside a road. He observed that some properly religious people crossed the road to avoid involvement. One passer-by, a despised member of another ethnic group, did stop and give aid. Jesus' question to his listeners is one of the important invitations to imagination in the history of religion. "Who is my neighbor?"

Lately, American politics have had a lot of huffing and puffing going on about moral behavior. A little moral imagination might help lift the whole tone of the political campaigns. Why not put oneself in the place of those left out of the American dream—poor children, unwed mothers, immigrants, prisoners—and by the use of imagination wonder what sort of community we could build.

Charles Dickens's *A Christmas Carol* is a wonderful story about what happens when someone begins to live inside the life of another through imagination. And what of the Christmas story itself? At its center is the outrageous suggestion that God, by a mighty act of imagination, came to live with us as a helpless baby.

Christian theology suggests that God's act of imagination in the Incarnation needs to be answered by risking ourselves in imagining the being of others in need of hope. Think about this as you walk the streets of your town this Christmas season.

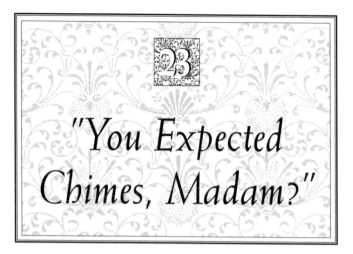

"You Expected Chimes, Madam?"

The details of belief are not as important as the uses of belief. This may seem somewhat outrageous at first glance. Religious folk can be so fond of particular details about their belief that the details overwhelm the purposes of belief.

Reinhold Niebuhr was a great theologian of the American church. He once suggested that some Christians worry too much about the "geography of heaven and hell, and the furniture of one and the temperature of the other." History is unfortunately full of terrible episodes of Christian people behaving in thoroughly un-Christian ways in order to make others "Christian."

Paul Tillich, another great theologian, described this kind of belief as opaque. There is so much accretion and self-interest overlaid on our religion that we cannot see through to the original power of the event. This is one of the risks of celebrating Christmas in a time of vast commercialism.

The religious traditions of Christianity that matter are not preliminary issues like how bishops dress or which confession the laity should honor. There are those who find the ordination of women to be so troubling to them that it makes it impossible to sense the heart of faith.

Christianity rejects opacity and celebrates transparency. Christmas is the most transparent holiday of faith. Yet even Christmas is at risk. It takes some concentration to focus our attention on the meaning behind the fragile character of the Incarnation.

A Christmas card manufacturer once told me that the most popular cards are those that reflect an outsider's view of the birth of Jesus. The shepherds looking into the stable is a popular theme. The Magi peering around the edge of the door is another. Do we have a problem breaking through the opaque barriers to full acceptance of the event?

There was a particularly funny moment in an old film you may remember. Monty Woolley was dressed as Santa Claus at a party and was slightly intoxicated. Unexpectedly he burped! A shocked matron gasped as she held her gloved hand to her mouth in disbelief. "You expected chimes, Madam?" said Monty Woolley's Santa Claus.

Monty Woolley's remark belongs with some of the more powerful proclamations of prophetic religion. Prophetic religion has basically one theme. We do not hear the powerful word of God because we have become comfortable with opacity—the density and piety of our lives that insulate us from events. In other words, we have grown comfortable with "chimes," embellishments that obscure and distract.

The wonder of Christmas is the persistence of the possibility of transparency. God comes to us in the form of an infant. All of the panoply of religious embellishment and political significance and personal pride are on hold. We have to deal with that.

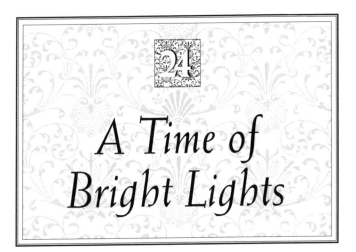

A Time of Bright Lights

Flying into a city these weeks before Christmas is a treat for even the most jaded traveler. The city is awash in light. Every neighborhood is outlined in the colors of holiday lights stretched over roofs and chimneys. This "Santa Claus view" of things is repeated all over the nation.

Christmas is a time of bright lights. We illuminate everything. Trees, houses, businesses, even skyscrapers. The metaphor of light is the dominant theme of Christmas.

Like so many other lovely themes surrounding Christmas, we have tended to lose the metaphor's intention. The beauty of the display is sufficient reason for good feelings. The tradition of stringing lights on tree and house is in itself a rite of family affection. Even for the Scrooges of the world, the gaiety and brightness are at least suggestive of something important.

GOD IS WITH US

But let's revisit the metaphor. It will help us understand the meaning of Christmas in the hopes of generations of faithful folk.

Try to imagine yourself in a prehistoric time. Your life would probably be circumscribed by the cycles of day and night—light and darkness. The day would be a time of activity and enterprise. But the night would be a time of anxiety and fear. Day provides perspective on events. Night obscures danger. Daytime suggests order. Nighttime hints at confusion.

The first act of creation according to the account in Genesis 1 was God's announcement: "Let there be light!" This was the introduction of meaning into the world. This was the beginning of hope and purpose and thought. Darkness was associated with the absence of hope and purpose and thought. Indeed, darkness became understood as the epitome of all that was not God, namely evil.

The early Christians, contemplating the powerful presence of Jesus, remembered the great claim in Genesis that the first act of creation was the establishment of light. They even called Jesus "the light of the world."

While the world seemed to be shrouded in darkness, their Lord came to throw light on events. Remembering the Genesis account, the author of the Gospel of John boldly asserted that "the light shines in the darkness, and the darkness did not overcome it."

Ah, there is the connection! The light still shines. Christmas is the time to celebrate the light. Behind all the splendor of Christmas lights there is the ancient affirmation that God is still at work in the world. This remains the hope of believers. No matter how dark the times may be, the light still shines.

It may be difficult for folk to understand this. Those caught in terrible moments of trauma or accident struggle with darkness. Those for whom life's promise seems to have passed them by wonder at the justice of it all. Folk who see no hope for rescue from disappointment may question the lights.

But for those who seek a way out of the darkness of despair, the lights of Christmas are a metaphor for the hope of the world. Even in the darkest of times, the light will not be extinguished. It will be visible for all who have eyes of faith.

Sophisticated modern folk have some difficulty with traditional religion. Christmas is a time when we come about as close to our religious roots as our urbanity will permit. But when darkness overwhelms, we turn toward the light. Then it is time to take stock.

Arthur Koestler was a man disillusioned by the heavy promises of Communism. He turned away from the politics of ideology when he saw what the arrogance of the state was doing to human beings. The book he later wrote about his struggle for human value and meaning was entitled *Darkness at Noon*.

When the glitzy and enticing promises of modernity grow dark in one's spirit, then it is time to look for the light. All the lights around town proclaim that faith even if they were hung by folk who have forgotten the metaphor.

❦

GOD IS WITH US

I Had to Come.
I Was Expected.

*I*srael has lived in the expectation that someday a great hero would come along and bring peace and salvation to the children of the land. This mighty dream has had the name of "Messiah." The Bible is filled with messianic stories and proclamations. There is a wide variation in the models of messiah. Israel has looked longingly at the Bible for hints about what they could expect.

Christians believe that the Messiah promised in the texts has already come to witness to the intentions of God. We look to Jesus.

The little band of Jesus' followers came to think of him as the Messiah when they tried to understand his ministry in the light of the biblical expectations. Many now forgotten religious or political leaders have been proclaimed as the "expected one." Other "messiahs" had been announced only to have been found wanting by Israel. Israel still longs for the expected one.

The Christians took the Greek word for "messiah" as the title for their lord. *Christos* is not a family name. To say "Jesus Christ" is to testify that Jesus of Nazareth is the Messiah-the Christ. The first followers even took the name to identify who they were—Chistians.

They proclaimed Jesus to be the long-awaited and promised one of Israel. The texts they found to confirm the lordship of Jesus were those that emphasized the strength of simplicity and the power of justice. The texts suggested that suffering would define faithfulness and that universal love rather than cultural pride would define messiahship.

The first Christians also introduced another element that changed the traditional views of the Messiah. Their Messiah would suffer, die, and rise again, but would also return to judge faithfulness and obedience to the ways of God. There was a touch of genius in their thinking. They knew that accountability was important because they knew their own limitations.

The first followers of Jesus were a nondescript ragtag group if there ever was one. They failed Jesus in his last hours. They quarreled over priority of place and prominence in his presence. And when he was arrested, they fled the city. The Easter experience gave them new power and confidence. That confirmed their expectations and they became new beings.

The expectation that God is always with us gives modern Christians moral and ethical power. The expected one, the Messiah, did not disappoint even when everyone disappointed him. That was no license for carelessness about responsibilities of faith. But it was an insight into the constancy of God. Expectation changes the land-scapes in which we work and live. We will be ready for the one who comes.

Joseph P. Lash tells a wonderful story about Eleanor Roosevelt in his biography of the great woman. She was advanced in years and not well. But she continued to fulfill a busy schedule of appointments. She had agreed to speak at a meeting in Harlem and it would have been understood if she had failed to appear. When she arrived at the hall where she was to speak, the hostess received her at curbside with the words, "I didn't think you would come." Mrs. Roosevelt replied, "I had to come. I was expected."

Jesus the Messiah and Jesus the babe in the manger come to us each Christmas. Jesus comes in the forms we expect and sometimes in shapes we have not expected. But the promise is clear. To those who expect him, he will come in all the manifold ways that our intelligence and imagination can provide. That is the Christmas story.

About the Author

F. Thomas Trotter is a consultant and is presently
serving as a part-time president of the Foundation for
United Methodist Communications, an agency related
to the General Commission on Communications of The
United Methodist Church. He served as president of
Alaska Pacific University in Anchorage from 1987–1995.
Prior to that position he was General Secretary of the
United Methodist Church's Board of Higher Education
in Nashville, Tennessee.

The author, a native of California, has served as

dean of Claremont School of Theology, chaplain of Boston University, a trustee for various colleges, and was the founder of the first private, church-related university in Zimbawe in 1984. He holds degrees from Occidental College, Boston University, and eight honorary degrees. He has published numerous articles and is the author of two books: *Jesus and the Historian* and *Loving God with One's Mind.*

Dr. Trotter is married to the former Gania Demaree, and they have three adult children: Ruth, Tania, and Mary.